Ronald Reagan

by Rosalyn Tucker

Consulting Editor: Gail Saunders-Smith, PhD

Consultant:
Sheila Blackford
Librarian, Scripps Library
Managing Editor, *American President*
Miller Center, University of Virginia

CAPSTONE PRESS
a capstone imprint

Pebble Plus is published by Capstone Press,
1710 Roe Crest Drive, North Mankato, Minnesota 56003
www.capstonepub.com

Library of Congress Cataloging-in-Publication Data
Tucker, Rosalyn.
 Ronald Reagan / by Rosalyn Tucker ; consulting editor, Gail Saunders-Smith, PhD ; consultant, Sheila Blackford, librarian, Scripps Library, managing editor, American President, Miller Center, University of Virginia.
pages cm. — (Pebble plus. presidential biographies)
Includes bibliographical references and index.
Summary: "Simple text and photographs present a biography of president Ronald Reagan"—Provided by publisher.
ISBN 978-1-4765-9613-6 (library binding)
ISBN 978-1-4765-9616-7 (paperback)
ISBN 978-1-4765-9679-8 (eBook PDF)
1. Reagan, Ronald—Juvenile literature. 2. Presidents—United States—Biography—Juvenile literature. 3. Motion picture actors and actresses—Biography—Juvenile literature. I. Title.
E877.T83 2014
973.927092—dc23
[B]   2013035611

Editorial Credits
Lori Bye, designer; Jo Miller, media researcher; Jennifer Walker, production specialist

Photo Credits
Corbis, 19; Courtesy Ronald Reagan Library, 5, 7, 9, 11; DoD, cover; Getty Images: John T. Barr, 15; NARA, 21; Newscom: ZUMA Press/Ronald Reagan Library, 17, ZUMA Press/Sacramento Bee, 13

Note to Parents and Teachers

The Presidential Biographies set supports national history standards related to people and culture. This book describes and illustrates the life of Ronald Reagan. The images support early readers in understanding the text. The repetition of words and phrases helps early readers learn new words. This book also introduces early readers to subject-specific vocabulary words, which are defined in the Glossary section. Early readers may need assistance to read some words and to use the Table of Contents, Glossary, Read More, Internet Sites, and Index sections of the book.

Printed in the United States of America in North Mankato, Minnesota.
092013   007775CGS14

Table of Contents

Early Life

Future president Ronald Reagan was born February 6, 1911, in Tampico, Illinois. Ronald's family didn't have a lot of money, but they always helped people in need.

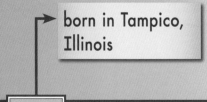

born in Tampico, Illinois

1911

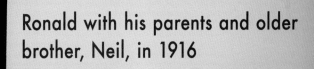

Ronald with his parents and older
brother, Neil, in 1916

In high school Ronald was friendly
and the other students liked him.
Ronald played on the football team.
He was also a good swimmer.
Ronald worked as a lifeguard
to save money for college.

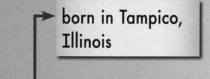

born in Tampico,
Illinois

1911

Ronald in 1927

Young Adult

Ronald went to Eureka College after high school. He acted in college plays and liked student politics. Ronald worked as a sports announcer after college.

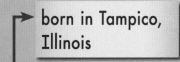

born in Tampico, Illinois

1911

9

In 1937 Ronald became an actor.

He was in more than 50 movies

and television shows. But Ronald

was never a big star. He met Nancy

Davis in 1951. Ronald and

Nancy got married a year later.

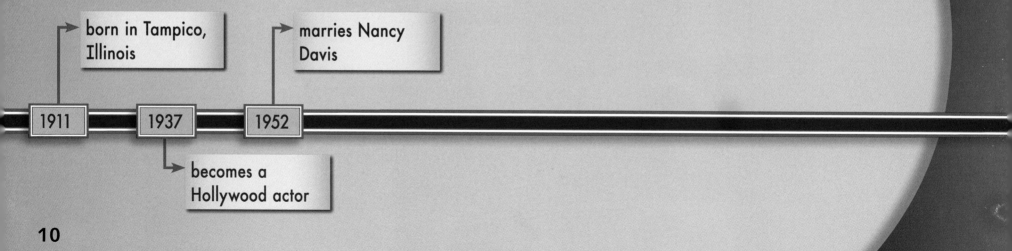

born in Tampico,
Illinois

marries Nancy
Davis

| 1911 | 1937 | 1952 |

becomes a
Hollywood actor

Ronald and Nancy on their wedding day in 1952

Life in California

Ronald decided to stop acting.

He wanted to work in politics.

In 1966 Ronald was elected

governor of California. He was

re-elected for another four years

in 1970.

born in Tampico,
Illinois

marries Nancy
Davis

1911   1937   1952   1966

becomes a
Hollywood actor

elected governor
of California

Ronald learned that compromising
with others helped get many
of his ideas turned into laws.
He remembered this lesson for
his next job. Ronald decided
to run for president in 1980.

born in Tampico,
Illinois

marries Nancy
Davis

1911   1937   1952   1966

becomes a
Hollywood actor

elected governor
of California

President Reagan

Ronald became the 40th U.S. president in 1981. He worked to make the government smaller and the military stronger. Ronald also tried to improve relations with the Soviet Union.

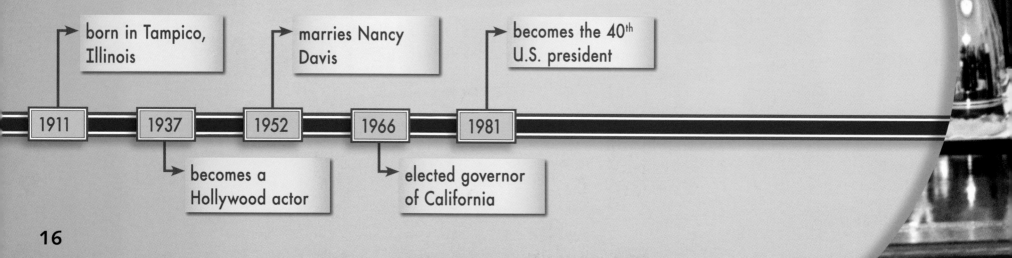

1911 — born in Tampico, Illinois

1937 — becomes a Hollywood actor

1952 — marries Nancy Davis

1966 — elected governor of California

1981 — becomes the 40th U.S. president

Ronald in 1982

Ronald was shot on March 30, 1981.
The man who shot him hurt three
other people. Everyone survived.
Ronald was back to work as president
in a few weeks.

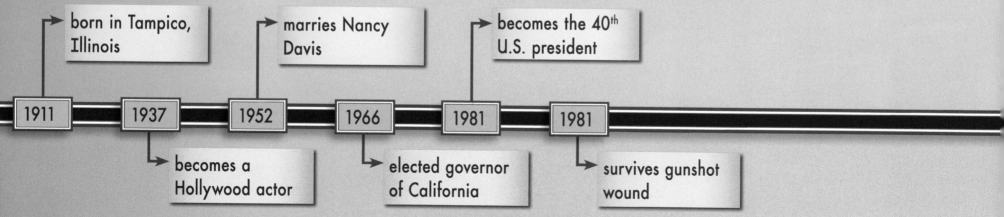

born in Tampico,
Illinois

marries Nancy
Davis

becomes the 40th
U.S. president

1911   1937   1952   1966   1981   1981

becomes a
Hollywood actor

elected governor
of California

survives gunshot
wound

GET WELL SOON
Mr. President
Jim, Tim, and Tom

Ronald in April 1981

Ronald left the White House after eight years as president. He died on June 5, 2004. Ronald always worked well with others. Today people remember Ronald as the "Great Communicator."

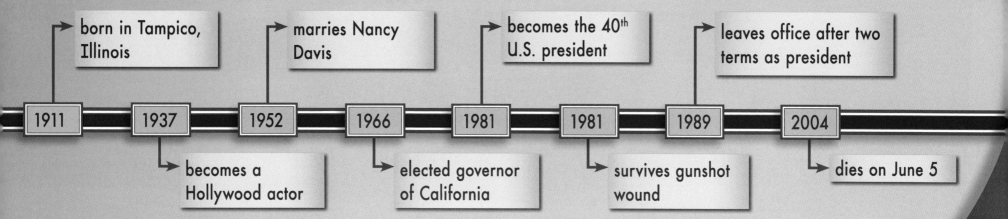

| 1911 | 1937 | 1952 | 1966 | 1981 | 1981 | 1989 | 2004 |

born in Tampico, Illinois

marries Nancy Davis

becomes the 40th U.S. president

leaves office after two terms as president

becomes a Hollywood actor

elected governor of California

survives gunshot wound

dies on June 5

Glossary

compromise—to agree to something that is not exactly what you wanted in order to make a decision

elect—to choose someone as a leader by voting

governor—a person chosen to be the head of a state's government

lifeguard—a person trained to help swimmers

military—the armed forces of a state or country

politics—the act of governing a city, state, or country

relations—the way people, countries, or organizations get along together

Soviet Union—a former group of 15 republics that included Russia, Ukraine, and other nations in eastern Europe and northern Asia

sports announcer—a person who describes the action during a sports event

Read More

Britton, Tamara L. *Ronald Reagan.* The United States Presidents. Edina, Minn.: ABDO Pub. Co., 2009.

Schuh, Mari C. *The U.S. Presidency.* The U.S. Government. Mankato, Minn.: Capstone Press, 2012.

Sutcliffe, Jane. *Ronald Reagan.* History Maker Bios. Minneapolis: Lerner Publications Co., 2008.

Internet Sites

FactHound offers a safe, fun way to find Internet sites related to this book. All of the sites on FactHound have been researched by our staff.

Here's all you do:

Visit *www.facthound.com*

Type in this code: 9781476596136

Super-cool stuff! Check out projects, games and lots more at **www.capstonekids.com**

Critical Thinking Using the Common Core

1. Ronald Reagan compromised with others to get his ideas turned into laws. What does it mean to compromise? Describe a time when you compromised. (Key Ideas and Details)

2. Ronald Reagan was called the "Great Communicator." What does it mean to be a communicator? Why is communication an important skill for the president? (Integration of Knowledge and Ideas)

3. Look at the photo on page 9. What does it show Ronald doing? Describe the clues in the photo that helped you figure out your answer. (Craft and Structure)

Index

Word Count: 270

Grade: 1

Early-Intervention Level: 22